AI Neuroplasticity

How Artificial Intelligence Reprograms the Brain to Learn, Heal & Adapt

By Joe Correa

Published by Live Stronger Faster

This book is for educational and informational purposes only. The author and publisher are not engaged in rendering legal, financial, or other professional advice. Readers should consult a qualified professional before making any financial decisions.

First Edition

Table of Contents

Introduction

The human brain has long been viewed as a fixed biological machine, shaped early in life and gradually declining with age, injury, or disease. For decades, neuroscience taught that once certain neural pathways were damaged or lost, recovery was limited at best. Learning slowed, memory weakened, habits hardened, and healing became increasingly difficult over time. Yet this view has quietly collapsed under the weight of modern research. We now know that the brain is not static, but dynamic—constantly reorganizing, adapting, and rewiring itself in response to experience. This phenomenon, known as neuroplasticity, is the foundation of learning, recovery, creativity, and resilience. What is new—and profoundly transformative—is the role artificial intelligence now plays in accelerating, guiding, and amplifying this natural capacity. AI is no longer merely a tool we use externally; it is becoming an active partner in shaping how the human brain learns, heals, and evolves.

Neuroplasticity is the brain's ability to change its structure and function based on input. Every thought, habit, emotion, movement, and repeated behavior strengthens certain neural connections while weakening others. This process has always been happening quietly in the background of daily life, driven by repetition, feedback, and attention. What artificial intelligence introduces is precision, personalization, and scale. AI systems can now analyze cognitive patterns, behavioral data, speech, movement, emotional responses, and performance metrics in real time, then adapt feedback loops that encourage the brain to form healthier, more efficient neural pathways. Instead of relying on generic training, guesswork, or slow trial-and-error learning, AI allows the brain to receive targeted stimulation optimized for its unique wiring, needs, and goals.

This book begins a journey into a new era of brain science—one where learning is faster, recovery is more achievable, and adaptation is continuous. AI-driven neuroplasticity does not replace the brain's natural intelligence; it enhances it. By identifying patterns invisible to human perception, artificial intelligence can detect when the brain is stuck in maladaptive loops—whether those loops manifest as poor focus, anxiety, cognitive fatigue, slow learning, or impaired recovery after trauma. Once identified, AI can help redirect attention, repetition, and feedback in ways that gently but persistently reshape neural circuits. The result is not forced change, but guided evolution—where the brain is nudged toward healthier configurations through consistent, data-driven interaction.

One of the most important shifts AI brings to neuroplasticity is the move from reactive care to proactive brain optimization. Traditionally, cognitive training, rehabilitation, and therapy were applied only after problems became severe—after a stroke, injury, diagnosis, or noticeable decline. AI changes this paradigm by making brain rewiring continuous and preventative. Algorithms can now monitor subtle changes in attention, memory, reaction time, emotional regulation, and mental fatigue long before symptoms become disruptive. These early signals allow AI systems to adjust training protocols, learning environments, and mental workloads in real time, helping the brain maintain balance rather than recover from breakdown. This shift has profound implications not only for medicine, but for education, productivity, mental health, and longevity.

AI-powered brain training systems are already demonstrating how adaptive feedback accelerates learning. Instead of presenting static content, these systems adjust difficulty, pacing, repetition, and sensory input based on how the brain responds moment by moment. When a learner struggles, the algorithm slows down, reframes information, or introduces supportive cues. When mastery increases, the system challenges the brain just enough to trigger growth without overload. This mirrors the optimal conditions for neuroplasticity identified by neuroscience: focused attention, emotional engagement, immediate feedback, and progressive challenge. AI simply ensures those conditions are met with far greater consistency than traditional methods ever allowed.

The implications of AI-driven neuroplasticity extend far beyond learning speed or academic performance. Habit formation, emotional regulation, decision-making, creativity, and self-control are all rooted in neural circuitry shaped by repetition and feedback. AI systems designed for behavioral change can identify patterns of avoidance, impulsivity, stress reactivity, or cognitive rigidity and help retrain those responses through subtle, repeated interventions. Over time, the brain begins to default to healthier patterns—not through willpower alone, but through rewired pathways that make better choices feel natural rather than forced. This is the quiet power of neuroplasticity when guided intelligently.

Healing is perhaps the most compelling frontier of AI-enabled neuroplasticity. After injury, stroke, or neurological disruption, the brain must reroute functions through alternative pathways. This process is possible at any age, but it is often slow and incomplete without proper guidance. AI systems can now analyze motor output, speech patterns, reaction timing, and neural signals to determine which pathways are compensating effectively and which are struggling. Training protocols can then be adjusted dynamically to encourage more efficient rewiring. The result is a more responsive rehabilitation process—one that adapts daily, even hourly, to the brain's changing capabilities. This approach transforms recovery from a rigid program into a living dialogue between brain and machine.

It is important to clarify what this book is—and what it is not. AI neuroplasticity is not about surrendering human agency to machines, nor is it about turning the brain into a programmable device stripped of individuality. On the contrary, AI works best when it amplifies human uniqueness. Each brain is different, shaped by genetics, experience, culture, and environment. Artificial intelligence allows training, learning, and healing to respect that individuality rather than force uniform solutions. When designed ethically and thoughtfully, AI becomes a mirror that reflects how the brain actually works, helping individuals engage with their own cognition more effectively.

This first book lays the conceptual and scientific groundwork for the entire series. It explains how neuroplasticity functions at a fundamental level and why artificial intelligence is uniquely suited to influence it. Subsequent books will explore specific applications—healing, mental health, performance, sleep, longevity, neurotechnology, and beyond—but all of those advances rest on the principles introduced here.

Understanding how the brain rewires itself, and how AI can guide that process, is essential to navigating the future of human cognition. We are entering a period where cognitive decline is no longer an inevitable consequence of aging, where recovery is not limited by outdated assumptions, and where learning can continue throughout life with unprecedented efficiency. AI does not make the brain artificial; it makes it more adaptable. It accelerates what the brain already does naturally when given the right conditions. The partnership between human neuroplasticity and artificial intelligence represents one of the most significant shifts in the history of human development—not because it changes who we are, but because it expands what we are capable of becoming.

As you move forward through this book and the series that follows, you are not simply reading about technology or neuroscience. You are engaging with a new framework for understanding the mind itself—one where intelligence is fluid, healing is ongoing, and growth does not have an expiration date. AI neuroplasticity is not a future concept; it is already shaping how we learn, recover, and adapt. The question is no longer whether the brain can change, but how intentionally—and how powerfully—we choose to guide that change.

Chapter 1

The Mechanics of Neuroplasticity in the Age of Artificial Intelligence

Neuroplasticity is not a metaphor, nor is it a motivational concept designed to inspire change through belief alone. It is a measurable biological process governed by synaptic strengthening, neural pruning, network reorganization, and functional reassignment within the brain. Every time a human being learns something new, practices a skill, reacts emotionally, or repeats a habit, neurons communicate across synapses, reinforcing certain pathways while allowing others to weaken. This process occurs continuously across the lifespan, not only during childhood as once believed. What artificial intelligence introduces into this natural system is not novelty, but amplification. AI increases the speed, precision, and consistency with which neuroplastic changes occur by shaping the conditions under which the brain learns, adapts, and heals.

At the cellular level, neuroplasticity depends on repetition, feedback, and attention. Neurons that fire together wire together, while unused connections fade through synaptic pruning. Traditionally, humans relied on conscious effort, coaching, therapy, or environmental exposure to drive these changes. The limitation of those methods has always been scale and personalization. No two brains respond identically to the same stimulus, yet most training, rehabilitation, and educational systems have been built around standardized inputs. Artificial intelligence disrupts this limitation by continuously observing performance data and modifying stimuli in response to how the brain actually behaves, not how it is expected to behave.

AI-driven neuroplastic systems function by creating adaptive feedback loops. These loops measure outputs such as reaction time, accuracy, emotional tone, speech patterns, motor coordination, decision latency, and cognitive fatigue. The system then adjusts variables—difficulty, pacing, repetition frequency, sensory input, or framing—to keep the brain operating within its optimal plasticity window. Too little challenge produces stagnation. Too much challenge produces stress and disengagement. AI excels at maintaining the precise balance required for sustained neural growth because it can make micro-adjustments far faster than any human instructor or therapist.

One of the most important principles of neuroplasticity is that the brain prioritizes efficiency over correctness. Neural pathways that reduce energy consumption and cognitive load become dominant, even if they are maladaptive. This explains why habits, fears, biases, and unproductive thought patterns are so persistent. AI systems designed for cognitive and behavioral change can detect these efficiency-driven loops and introduce alternative pathways that are gradually reinforced through repetition and reward. Over time, the brain adopts these new routes not because it is forced to, but because they become energetically favorable. This is how AI-assisted rewiring differs fundamentally from willpower-based change.

Artificial intelligence also expands neuroplasticity by extending feedback beyond conscious awareness. Humans are limited in their ability to self-monitor subtle changes in cognition or emotion. AI can track patterns across days, weeks, and months, identifying correlations between sleep, stress, learning performance, emotional regulation, and environmental factors. These insights allow for interventions that occur before breakdown, burnout, or regression. Instead of responding to failure, AI enables preemptive optimization. The brain is guided gently back toward balance before maladaptive patterns fully consolidate.

Another critical mechanism of AI-driven neuroplasticity is multimodal stimulation. The brain integrates information across sensory, cognitive, and emotional domains. AI systems can coordinate visual, auditory, linguistic, and kinesthetic inputs simultaneously, reinforcing neural connections across multiple regions. This cross-network engagement accelerates learning and retention while reducing cognitive fatigue. When properly designed, AI does not overwhelm the brain; it synchronizes stimulation to match neural readiness, creating conditions under which change feels natural rather than forced.

Neuroplasticity is also deeply influenced by emotional state. Stress hormones inhibit plasticity, while curiosity, safety, and intrinsic motivation enhance it. AI systems can infer emotional states through voice, language patterns, facial expression, or physiological data and adjust interactions accordingly. When frustration rises, the system can slow down or reframe tasks. When engagement increases, it can introduce complexity. This emotional responsiveness transforms AI from a static tool into a dynamic partner in cognitive development.

Importantly, AI does not replace human learning processes; it scaffolds them. The brain remains the agent of change. Artificial intelligence simply provides a mirror that reflects performance with greater clarity and consistency than human perception allows. Over time, users internalize improved learning strategies, emotional regulation techniques, and cognitive habits. The ultimate goal of AI-assisted neuroplasticity is not dependency, but autonomy—training the brain so effectively that it requires less external guidance over time. As AI continues to evolve, its role in neuroplasticity will expand from passive guidance to predictive modeling. Systems will increasingly anticipate when the brain is approaching overload, stagnation, or decline and intervene automatically. This predictive capacity represents a shift from episodic training to continuous neural maintenance. Just as physical fitness benefits from ongoing conditioning rather than sporadic effort, cognitive health will increasingly rely on adaptive, AI-guided engagement across the lifespan.

This chapter establishes the foundational mechanics that underpin the entire series. AI-driven neuroplasticity is not speculative science; it is an extension of well-established neurological principles enhanced by data, computation, and adaptive feedback. Understanding these mechanics is essential for appreciating how AI can support healing, emotional regulation, performance, longevity, and even consciousness itself. With this foundation in place, the remainder of this book and series explores what becomes possible when the brain's natural adaptability is guided intelligently and ethically.

"The Day the Brain Learned How to Learn Again"

When Daniel first noticed something was wrong, it wasn't dramatic. There was no accident, no diagnosis, no sudden collapse. It began with hesitation. Words lingered just out of reach. Simple decisions felt heavier than they used to. His focus drifted after minutes instead of hours. At forty-six, he told himself it was stress, overwork, maybe age. But the unease grew quietly, like a background hum he couldn't turn off.

Daniel had built his career on problem-solving. He was methodical, analytical, dependable. Yet tasks that once felt effortless now demanded deliberate effort. He reread emails twice before sending them. He forgot names moments after hearing them. Most unsettling was the sense that his mind was resisting itself, as if familiar pathways were eroding beneath his thoughts. He tried productivity apps, memory exercises, meditation videos. Nothing stuck. Improvement came in flashes, then faded.

It wasn't until a colleague mentioned an AI-based cognitive training program that Daniel felt a flicker of curiosity. He was skeptical. He didn't believe a system could understand his mind better than he did. Still, the program promised something different—not generic exercises, but adaptive training that adjusted to how his brain responded in real time. There were no claims of instant transformation, only consistency. Daniel decided to try it, expecting little.

The first sessions felt strangely unremarkable. The tasks were simple—pattern recognition, reaction timing, short memory sequences. Yet something subtle was happening beneath the surface. The system adjusted itself constantly. When Daniel hesitated, it slowed. When his responses sharpened, it challenged him. He noticed that frustration never escalated the way it used to. Just as he felt himself slipping, the task shifted, keeping him engaged without strain.

Over days, then weeks, the changes accumulated quietly. Daniel found himself finishing tasks with less mental friction. His focus extended naturally. Decisions no longer felt heavy; they flowed. The program didn't tell him he was improving. It simply reflected his performance back to him, adapting as his brain adapted. For the first time in years, learning felt fluid again.

What surprised Daniel most was that the improvements extended beyond the sessions. Conversations became easier. His memory stabilized. The mental fog lifted gradually, not as a sudden breakthrough but as a steady clearing. He realized that his brain hadn't been failing him—it had been stuck in inefficient loops reinforced by stress and repetition. The AI system hadn't fixed him; it had redirected his attention and feedback long enough for his brain to rewire itself.

One evening, months later, Daniel noticed something else. He no longer relied on the system as much. The strategies it had reinforced—pausing, reframing, pacing—had become internal habits. His brain had learned how to learn again. The technology that once guided him had quietly stepped back, its work embedded in the neural pathways it helped strengthen.

Daniel understood then that the future of intelligence wasn't about replacing the human mind. It was about reminding it of its own adaptability. AI hadn't given him a new brain. It had given his brain the conditions it needed to remember what it was always capable of doing.

Chapter 2

How Artificial Intelligence Trains the Brain Through Feedback, Adaptation, and Precision

Neuroplastic change does not occur simply because information is presented to the brain. It occurs when the brain receives feedback that is timely, relevant, and emotionally tolerable enough to sustain engagement. For most of human history, feedback has been slow, inconsistent, and generalized. A teacher might notice confusion after a test, a therapist might adjust an approach after weeks, or an individual might recognize failure only after repeated frustration. Artificial intelligence transforms this process by collapsing the feedback loop. Instead of waiting for outcomes, AI responds to signals as they occur, shaping neural activity while it is still forming.

The brain learns best when feedback arrives at the moment of action. This timing allows synapses to strengthen or weaken in direct association with the behavior that triggered them. AI systems excel at delivering this immediacy. Whether the task involves memory recall, motor coordination, emotional regulation, or attention control, algorithms can measure performance in milliseconds and respond instantly. This creates a learning environment where the brain is continuously guided toward more efficient configurations without conscious effort or delay.

Adaptation is the second critical element. Static systems assume the brain remains the same from one moment to the next, but neuroplasticity is inherently dynamic. Fatigue, stress, motivation, and emotional state fluctuate constantly, altering how the brain processes information. Artificial intelligence accommodates this variability by adjusting parameters in real time. When cognitive load increases, the system reduces complexity. When engagement rises, it introduces challenge. This constant recalibration keeps the brain within its optimal zone for plasticity, avoiding both overload and stagnation.

Precision distinguishes AI-guided learning from traditional methods. Instead of broad categories such as "beginner" or "advanced," AI models learning at a granular level. They detect micro-patterns in response speed, error type, hesitation, and recovery. These signals reveal not just what the brain gets wrong, but how it processes information. Training can then target the specific neural bottleneck rather than applying generic repetition. This precision accelerates learning while reducing frustration and cognitive fatigue. Another defining feature of AI-driven neuroplasticity is consistency. Human-guided training is subject to variability in mood, attention, and availability. AI systems deliver stable, repeatable conditions that reinforce neural pathways reliably over time. Consistency does not mean rigidity; it means dependable adaptation governed by objective data rather than subjective judgment. This reliability allows small improvements to compound into lasting neural change.

Feedback is not limited to correctness. AI systems increasingly incorporate emotional and physiological signals into their models. Voice tone, facial expression, language choice, heart rate variability, and response latency provide insight into the brain's internal state. By integrating these signals, AI can adjust not only the task but the manner in which it is presented. A reframed instruction, a brief pause, or a shift in modality can preserve engagement and prevent stress from inhibiting plasticity.

One of the most powerful aspects of AI-guided feedback is its ability to reveal progress that humans might overlook. Neuroplastic change often occurs gradually, below the threshold of conscious awareness. AI systems track these incremental shifts, reinforcing motivation by demonstrating improvement objectively. This transparency strengthens engagement and trust, encouraging sustained participation long enough for neural restructuring to take hold. Importantly, AI does not dictate outcomes; it shapes conditions. The brain remains responsible for forming and stabilizing new connections. Artificial intelligence simply ensures that the signals driving those connections are optimized. Over time, the brain internalizes these optimized patterns, requiring less external guidance. The ultimate measure of success is not dependence on AI, but the transfer of improved learning strategies into daily cognition.

As AI systems become more sophisticated, feedback loops will extend beyond isolated training sessions into everyday environments. Learning, work, recovery, and rest will increasingly be guided by adaptive systems that respond continuously to cognitive and emotional signals. This integration represents a shift from episodic intervention to ongoing neural stewardship. Understanding how feedback, adaptation, and precision interact is essential to grasping how AI reshapes the brain's capacity to learn, heal, and adapt across the lifespan.

"The Algorithm That Listened"

Maria had always thought of feedback as something external, usually arriving too late to matter. In school, it came as grades weeks after effort. At work, it arrived during annual reviews that summarized months of missed opportunities. Even in therapy, progress felt abstract, discussed after the fact rather than felt in the moment. When she enrolled in an AI-guided emotional regulation program, she expected more of the same—insight delivered after struggle.

Instead, the system felt oddly attentive. It didn't ask her how she felt; it listened. As Maria spoke, the software tracked subtle shifts in her voice. When her breathing tightened, the interface slowed. When her words became sharper, prompts softened. Nothing was announced. Nothing was corrected outright. The conversation simply adjusted itself around her.

At first, Maria found this unsettling. She was used to pushing through discomfort, forcing calm where it didn't exist. The AI didn't allow that. Each time her stress spiked, the system altered the interaction just enough to keep her engaged without escalation. It felt as if the conversation itself was breathing with her.

Over time, Maria noticed that her reactions were changing. Situations that once triggered immediate defensiveness now produced a pause. She felt herself noticing emotional shifts before they peaked. The system wasn't telling her what to feel; it was showing her when she was about to lose balance and gently redirecting her attention.

Weeks passed, and Maria began to anticipate the adjustments. She recognized the signals herself—the tightening chest, the sharper tone—and responded before the system needed to.

The feedback loop that once existed externally had begun to internalize. Her brain was learning from the rhythm of interaction rather than the content alone.

One evening, during a stressful conversation with a family member, Maria realized she was applying the same pacing instinctively. She slowed her speech. She reframed her thoughts. The moment passed without escalation. There was no system present, no prompts, no interface. Yet the training was there, embedded in her responses.

Maria understood then that the algorithm hadn't been controlling her emotions. It had been listening closely enough to help her brain hear itself. The feedback she had always needed wasn't judgment or advice—it was timing. And once her brain learned that rhythm, it no longer required the system to maintain it.

Chapter 3

Rewiring Attention, Focus, and Cognitive Control With Artificial Intelligence

Attention is the gateway to neuroplasticity. The brain cannot rewire what it does not attend to, and it cannot sustain change without repeated focus over time. Modern cognitive decline is not primarily caused by a lack of intelligence, but by fragmented attention. Constant stimulation, multitasking, emotional overload, and digital distraction have trained the brain to switch rapidly rather than sustain engagement. This shift has weakened the neural circuits responsible for focus, impulse control, and deep thinking. Artificial intelligence introduces a counterforce by retraining attention itself, not through discipline or restriction, but through adaptive cognitive scaffolding.

The brain's attention system is governed by competing neural networks. Some networks prioritize novelty and rapid response, while others support sustained concentration and executive control. When novelty-driven networks dominate, focus becomes shallow and reactive. AI systems can detect this imbalance by analyzing response patterns such as rapid task-switching, declining accuracy over time, impulsive input, and delayed recovery after distraction. Once detected, AI adjusts task structure, pacing, and stimulation to encourage longer engagement periods without triggering fatigue or frustration.

One of the most effective ways AI strengthens attention is by reducing cognitive friction. When tasks are poorly aligned with the brain's current capacity, attention collapses. AI-driven systems continuously recalibrate difficulty so that effort feels purposeful rather than draining. This alignment keeps the brain engaged long enough for neural circuits associated with focus to strengthen. Over time, sustained attention becomes less effortful because the underlying networks have been reinforced through repeated success.

Cognitive control—the ability to regulate impulses, manage competing demands, and maintain goal-directed behavior—is another critical target of AI-guided neuroplasticity. Traditional approaches rely heavily on conscious self-regulation, which is limited and exhaustible. AI systems reduce reliance on willpower by shaping environments that naturally support control. By timing prompts, structuring choices, and sequencing tasks intelligently, AI minimizes decision fatigue and reinforces executive function indirectly. Artificial intelligence also retrains attention by managing cognitive load.

The brain has a finite capacity for processing information. When overloaded, it defaults to shortcuts that undermine learning and focus. AI monitors load indicators such as error frequency, response latency, and emotional cues, then adjusts input accordingly. This dynamic load management allows the brain to remain engaged without tipping into stress, preserving the neurochemical conditions required for plasticity.

Another important mechanism is attentional feedback. Humans are often unaware of when their attention drifts. AI systems provide subtle cues—changes in task flow, visual emphasis, or pacing—that redirect focus without interruption. These micro-corrections teach the brain to recognize and recover from distraction more quickly. Over time, recovery becomes automatic, reducing the duration and impact of attentional lapses.

AI-guided focus training also benefits from pattern recognition across time. By analyzing longitudinal data, AI identifies when attention is strongest and weakest throughout the day, week, or month. This allows cognitive work to be scheduled during optimal windows while recovery is prioritized during low-capacity periods. Aligning effort with natural rhythms prevents burnout and supports long-term cognitive resilience.

As focus improves, downstream effects emerge across memory, learning speed, emotional regulation, and creativity. Sustained attention strengthens memory consolidation, enabling information to transfer from short-term processing to long-term storage. Emotional reactivity decreases as executive networks gain influence over limbic responses. Creative insight increases as the brain maintains engagement long enough to explore complex associations. These outcomes are not separate skills; they are expressions of a more stable attentional foundation.

The goal of AI-driven attention training is not constant focus, but flexible control. A healthy brain can shift attention intentionally, sustain it when needed, and disengage without residue. Artificial intelligence accelerates the development of this flexibility by guiding the brain through repeated cycles of engagement, recovery, and reinforcement. As these cycles accumulate, attention transforms from a scarce resource into a trained capacity.

This chapter establishes attention as a trainable function rather than a fixed trait. AI does not force focus; it teaches the brain how to access it reliably. By reshaping the conditions under which attention operates, artificial intelligence enables deeper learning, greater self-regulation, and more effective use of cognitive energy. With attention restored, the brain becomes receptive to the broader transformations explored throughout the remainder of this book and series.

"The Quiet Return of Focus"

Ethan hadn't noticed when his focus disappeared. It slipped away gradually, disguised as productivity. He answered messages constantly, switched tasks effortlessly, stayed busy from morning until night. Yet at the end of each day, he felt strangely unsatisfied, as if nothing meaningful had been completed. Reading felt impossible. Conversations drifted. His thoughts fractured before reaching depth.

When Ethan tried an AI-guided focus system, he expected rigid structure or aggressive productivity tactics. Instead, the system felt almost invisible. Tasks appeared simpler than expected, but they adapted constantly. When his attention wavered, the interface slowed. When his engagement deepened, it extended the challenge. There were no alarms, no scolding reminders—only subtle adjustments that kept him present.

At first, Ethan grew impatient. He wanted efficiency, speed, output. The system seemed unconcerned with speed. It prioritized continuity. Gradually, he noticed something unfamiliar: stillness. He could stay with a single task longer without effort. Distraction didn't vanish, but it lost its urgency. His mind no longer lunged at every stimulus.

Days turned into weeks, and the changes followed him beyond the system. Ethan found himself listening more fully in conversations. Reading no longer felt like a struggle. His thoughts unfolded in complete arcs rather than fragments. Focus wasn't forced—it emerged naturally, as if his brain had remembered an old skill.

One afternoon, while working on a complex problem, Ethan realized he had been immersed for over an hour without checking his phone. There was no strain, no tension. Just engagement. The system hadn't trained him to block distraction; it had trained his brain to value depth again.

When Ethan eventually reduced his use of the AI tool, the focus remained. The pathways had been reinforced. His brain had relearned how to stay. The noise of constant switching faded into the background, replaced by a quieter, more deliberate rhythm of thought.

Ethan understood then that focus wasn't something he had lost forever. It was something that had been neglected—and gently restored once the brain was given the right conditions to practice it again.

Chapter 4

Memory Formation, Learning Speed, and the AI-Driven Reinforcement of Neural Pathways

Memory is not a storage problem; it is a reinforcement problem. The brain does not retain information simply because it has been encountered, but because neural pathways associated with that information have been activated, stabilized, and revisited under the right conditions. Forgetting is not failure—it is the default state when reinforcement is insufficient. Artificial intelligence transforms memory formation by optimizing the timing, frequency, and context in which reinforcement occurs, aligning learning with how the brain naturally consolidates information.

Traditional learning assumes linear progression: information is presented, reviewed, tested, and repeated. The brain, however, learns nonlinearly. It strengthens memories through spaced repetition, emotional relevance, contextual variation, and sleep-dependent consolidation. AI systems model these biological processes and apply them dynamically. Instead of repeating content on a fixed schedule, AI identifies when a memory is at risk of decay and reintroduces it at precisely the moment reinforcement will be most effective. This timing strengthens synaptic connections while minimizing cognitive load.

Learning speed improves when the brain spends less energy guessing what matters. AI reduces noise by prioritizing signals. By analyzing performance data, AI systems determine which concepts are foundational and which are derivative, focusing reinforcement on the neural anchors that support broader understanding. This approach accelerates mastery by strengthening core pathways first, allowing related knowledge to attach more easily. The result is not just faster learning, but more durable understanding.

Memory is also state-dependent. The brain recalls information more effectively when internal conditions resemble those present during encoding. AI systems account for this by varying context deliberately. Concepts are revisited across different modalities, emotional states, and environments, preventing memories from becoming brittle or situational. This variability trains the brain to retrieve information flexibly, strengthening connections across networks rather than isolating them within narrow contexts.

Artificial intelligence further enhances memory by detecting interference. When similar pieces of information compete for the same neural real estate, confusion and forgetting increase. AI systems identify these collisions through error patterns and response delays, then separate reinforcement to prevent overlap. This reduces cognitive friction and preserves clarity, especially in complex learning domains.

Another critical function of AI-guided learning is retrieval practice. The act of recalling information strengthens memory more than passive review. AI systems encourage active retrieval by prompting recall at optimal intervals, adjusting difficulty based on success. When recall is too easy, reinforcement weakens. When it is too difficult, frustration inhibits plasticity. AI maintains the balance that keeps retrieval effortful but achievable, strengthening pathways efficiently.

Sleep plays a crucial role in memory consolidation, and AI systems increasingly incorporate sleep data into learning models. By aligning reinforcement schedules with sleep cycles, AI maximizes consolidation during slow-wave and REM phases. This integration reflects a shift toward holistic cognitive training—one that respects the biological rhythms underlying neuroplasticity.

Over time, AI-guided reinforcement reshapes how the brain approaches learning itself. Learners develop intuition for pacing, spacing, and engagement. The brain becomes more efficient at encoding new information because existing pathways provide stable scaffolding. Learning speed increases not because the brain works harder, but because it works with less resistance.

The broader implication is that memory and learning are not fixed capacities. They are dynamic processes that respond to environment, feedback, and timing. Artificial intelligence excels at managing these variables continuously, enabling the brain to retain more with less effort. As reinforcement becomes optimized, learning transforms from repetition into refinement, from memorization into integration.

This chapter establishes memory as a living system rather than a static archive. AI does not replace memory; it teaches the brain how to preserve what matters. With reinforced pathways in place, the brain becomes more resilient, adaptable, and prepared for the higher-order transformations explored throughout the remainder of this book.

"What Stayed This Time"

Lena had always been a fast learner—until she wasn't. Somewhere between professional demands and constant information intake, knowledge began slipping through her grasp. She could read an article in the morning and struggle to recall it by evening. Courses felt overwhelming. Ideas arrived briefly, then vanished. She blamed distraction, age, fatigue. None of the usual fixes worked.

When Lena started using an AI-driven learning system, she noticed something unexpected. The system didn't ask her to study more. It asked her to pause. Concepts returned at odd intervals, sometimes days later, sometimes in different formats. A question instead of a paragraph. An example instead of a definition. At first, she found it disorienting.

But gradually, something changed. Ideas began sticking. Not all at once, but quietly. She recognized concepts without strain. Connections formed between topics she had never linked before. Learning felt lighter, less forced. The system seemed to know when she was about to forget—and intervened just in time.

One night, Lena realized she was recalling information effortlessly during a conversation. There was no searching, no anxiety. The knowledge was simply there. She hadn't memorized it deliberately. It had settled into place.

Weeks later, she reduced her reliance on the system, expecting the gains to fade. They didn't. Her brain had adapted to the rhythm of reinforcement. She found herself revisiting ideas naturally, spacing learning without conscious planning. Lena understood then that memory wasn't about holding on tighter. It was about letting information return at the right moments. The AI hadn't stored knowledge for her—it had taught her brain when to invite it back.

Chapter 5

Emotional Regulation, Stress Response, and AI-Guided Neural Resilience

Emotional regulation is not a personality trait; it is a neurological skill shaped by experience, repetition, and context. The brain's emotional responses are governed by interconnected networks that evaluate threat, reward, memory, and meaning. When these networks become dysregulated—through chronic stress, trauma, or cognitive overload—the brain prioritizes survival over learning, narrowing attention and inhibiting neuroplasticity. Artificial intelligence plays a critical role in restoring balance by helping the brain recognize, modulate, and rewire emotional responses without suppressing them.

Stress fundamentally alters how the brain processes information. Elevated cortisol levels impair memory consolidation, reduce executive control, and bias perception toward threat. Traditional stress management techniques rely heavily on conscious awareness, which is often unavailable in moments of emotional escalation. AI systems bypass this limitation by detecting physiological and behavioral markers of stress before conscious recognition occurs. Changes in speech cadence, reaction time, facial tension, or decision latency provide early signals that the nervous system is shifting into a reactive state.

Once these signals are detected, AI systems adjust interactions to reduce emotional load. This may involve slowing task pacing, reframing information, or introducing brief recovery intervals. These micro-adjustments prevent stress from escalating to levels that inhibit plasticity. Over time, repeated exposure to regulated conditions retrains the brain's threat detection systems, reducing hypersensitivity and strengthening pathways associated with calm assessment and emotional flexibility.

Emotional regulation improves when the brain learns that not every stimulus requires immediate reaction. AI-guided systems reinforce this learning by introducing controlled pauses between stimulus and response. These pauses strengthen prefrontal networks responsible for impulse control and decision-making. As these networks gain influence, emotional responses become more proportionate and recover more quickly. The brain does not become emotionally numb; it becomes emotionally resilient.

Another key mechanism of AI-assisted regulation is pattern interruption. Many emotional reactions are habitual, triggered automatically by familiar cues. AI systems identify these patterns through repeated interactions and introduce subtle variations that disrupt automaticity. By changing timing, phrasing, or sensory context, AI prevents the brain from defaulting to entrenched responses. This creates space for alternative pathways to form, supporting more adaptive emotional processing.

AI also supports emotional regulation by reinforcing interoceptive awareness—the brain's ability to sense internal states. Through feedback loops that reflect physiological changes back to the user, AI helps individuals recognize emotional shifts earlier. This awareness strengthens self-regulation by enabling timely intervention before emotions escalate. Over time, the brain internalizes this monitoring capability, reducing dependence on external cues.

Consistency is essential for emotional rewiring. Sporadic regulation efforts produce limited results because emotional networks strengthen through repetition. AI systems provide stable, predictable environments that reinforce regulation consistently across contexts. This reliability allows the brain to generalize regulation skills beyond training sessions into daily life, supporting long-term resilience.

As emotional regulation improves, secondary benefits emerge across cognition. Attention stabilizes, memory retention increases, and learning accelerates as stress-related interference diminishes. The brain becomes more receptive to new information and more flexible in adapting to change. Emotional resilience thus serves as a foundation for broader neuroplastic growth.

The long-term goal of AI-guided emotional regulation is not emotional control, but emotional fluency. A resilient brain can experience emotion fully without becoming overwhelmed or rigid. Artificial intelligence facilitates this fluency by shaping the conditions under which emotional learning occurs, allowing the brain to practice regulation repeatedly in low-risk environments. Over time, regulation becomes intuitive rather than effortful.

This chapter underscores the inseparable relationship between emotion and learning. Neuroplasticity thrives in environments where emotional safety and challenge coexist. AI enables the precise calibration of these conditions, helping the brain rebuild trust in its own capacity to respond rather than react. With emotional resilience restored, the brain is prepared for deeper healing and higher-order adaptation explored throughout the remainder of this series.

"The Space Between the Feeling"

When Aaron felt overwhelmed, it happened fast. A single comment could ignite a cascade of thoughts, tightening his chest and narrowing his vision. He prided himself on logic, yet emotions bypassed reason entirely. By the time he realized he was reacting, the moment had already passed—and the damage with it.

Aaron didn't consider himself emotional. He considered himself efficient. But efficiency vanished whenever stress appeared. His responses felt automatic, as if someone else were steering. When he began using an AI-guided emotional regulation system, he didn't expect much. He assumed emotions were either controlled or uncontrollable.

The system never asked him to calm down. It simply changed the pace. Conversations slowed when his tone sharpened. Tasks softened when pressure rose. At first, Aaron found this irritating. He wanted to push through, not pause. But the pauses persisted—not long enough to interrupt, just long enough to notice.

Over time, something subtle emerged. A fraction of a second appeared between feeling and response. It wasn't dramatic, but it was new. In that space, Aaron could choose. Sometimes he still reacted—but often, he didn't.

Weeks passed, and the space widened. Stress still arrived, but it no longer hijacked him. His body signaled earlier. His thoughts slowed naturally. The system rarely intervened now; his brain had learned the rhythm.

One afternoon, during a tense meeting, Aaron felt the familiar surge rise. But instead of responding immediately, he paused. Just briefly. The moment passed without escalation. He realized afterward that the pause hadn't been forced. It had emerged instinctively.

The AI hadn't removed his emotions. It had taught his brain where to place space around them. In that space, Aaron discovered something unexpected—not control, but freedom.

Chapter 6

Habit Formation, Behavioral Change, and AI-Guided Neural Repatterning

Habits are not choices repeated; they are neural shortcuts refined over time. Once established, habits operate below conscious awareness, conserving cognitive energy by automating behavior. This efficiency is beneficial when habits are adaptive, but deeply limiting when they are not. Unproductive routines, compulsive behaviors, and self-sabotaging patterns persist not because of weakness, but because the brain has learned that these pathways are reliable. Artificial intelligence enables habit change by addressing the brain at the level where habits actually live: automated neural circuitry reinforced by repetition, reward, and context.

Behavioral change fails most often because it targets intention rather than structure. The brain does not change habits simply because it understands consequences. It changes when alternative pathways become easier, more rewarding, and more predictable than existing ones. AI systems identify the precise conditions under which habits activate by analyzing timing, emotional state, environmental cues, and behavioral sequences. Once these triggers are mapped, AI introduces subtle modifications that weaken the old loop while strengthening a new one.

Habit loops consist of three components: cue, routine, and reward. AI-guided systems intervene at all three points. They alter cues by changing timing or context, reshape routines by introducing alternative actions that satisfy the same underlying need, and recalibrate rewards by reinforcing adaptive outcomes more consistently than maladaptive ones. This process does not rely on resistance; it relies on replacement. The brain gradually adopts new pathways because they become the most efficient option available.

Consistency is essential in habit repatterning. Sporadic effort allows old circuits to remain dominant. AI systems excel at maintaining consistency by delivering reliable reinforcement across contexts and timeframes. Unlike human-guided change, which is influenced by mood and memory, AI applies interventions with unwavering regularity. This stability accelerates synaptic weakening of old habits while strengthening new connections.

Another critical advantage of AI in behavioral change is its ability to operate below conscious strain. Willpower is finite and easily exhausted. AI reduces the need for constant decision-making by shaping environments that naturally guide behavior. Choices are simplified, friction is reduced for adaptive actions, and obstacles are introduced for maladaptive ones. Over time, behavior shifts without sustained conscious effort, allowing change to persist even during stress or fatigue.

AI also detects relapse patterns early. Small deviations often precede full regression, but humans rarely notice them in time. AI systems identify subtle behavioral drift and intervene gently before old pathways reassert dominance. These early corrections prevent discouragement and maintain momentum, reinforcing the brain's confidence in its ability to change.

As new habits stabilize, the brain undergoes structural reorganization. Neural efficiency shifts toward adaptive routines, reducing the cognitive cost of maintaining change. What once required effort becomes automatic. At this stage, behavior feels natural rather than imposed, signaling successful neuroplastic repatterning.

The broader implication of AI-guided habit formation is that behavior is malleable at any stage of life. The brain remains capable of restructuring automated patterns when given consistent, targeted feedback. Artificial intelligence does not force discipline; it engineers conditions that make adaptive behavior inevitable. This chapter demonstrates that long-term change does not require constant struggle. It requires alignment between neural incentives and desired outcomes. AI provides that alignment by redesigning feedback loops at the level where habits form. With behavior repatterned, the brain becomes freer—less constrained by outdated routines and more responsive to intentional choice.

"The Habit That Let Go"

Nina had tried to change herself more times than she could count. She set goals, made plans, promised tomorrow would be different. And for a while, it was. Then stress arrived, routine returned, and the old behaviors reclaimed their place. Each attempt left her more convinced that some habits were permanent.

When Nina began using an AI-guided behavioral system, she didn't announce her goals. The system didn't ask her to. Instead, it watched. It noticed patterns she hadn't—when her energy dipped, when decisions became reactive, when familiar routines resurfaced. Nothing was labeled good or bad. It was simply mapped.

At first, the changes were barely noticeable. A reminder appeared earlier than expected. A task was rearranged. A pause emerged where none had existed before. Nina felt resistance—not because the changes were difficult, but because they disrupted familiarity. Still, she continued. Days passed, and something strange happened. The urge to repeat old behaviors weakened—not dramatically, but enough to hesitate. In that hesitation, alternatives appeared. The system didn't demand better choices; it made them easier.

Weeks later, Nina realized she was no longer fighting herself. The routines she wanted had begun happening on their own. The old habits hadn't vanished—they simply no longer felt inevitable.

One evening, after a stressful day that would have once triggered regression, Nina noticed she hadn't followed the old pattern. There was no triumph, no effort. Just a quiet deviation. The new routine had become the path of least resistance.

Nina understood then that the habit hadn't been broken—it had been replaced. Her brain had learned a new shortcut. And once learned, it no longer needed to be defended.

Chapter 7

Nervous System Reset, Recovery, and AI-Guided Neuroplastic Stabilization

Neuroplasticity cannot occur sustainably in a nervous system that remains locked in survival mode. While learning, habit change, and emotional regulation reshape neural pathways, long-term adaptation depends on the brain's ability to return to baseline after stimulation. Chronic stress, overstimulation, poor sleep, and constant cognitive demand keep the nervous system in a state of heightened alert, limiting plasticity and accelerating cognitive fatigue. Artificial intelligence plays a critical role in restoring balance by helping the brain recognize when to activate and when to recover, enabling stabilization rather than continuous strain.

The autonomic nervous system governs this balance through two complementary branches. One mobilizes energy for action, while the other restores equilibrium through rest and repair. Modern environments bias the system toward persistent activation, leaving little opportunity for recovery. AI-guided systems detect this imbalance by analyzing physiological signals such as heart rate variability, breathing patterns, reaction consistency, and cognitive endurance. These indicators reveal when the nervous system is overextended, even when conscious awareness is absent.

Once imbalance is detected, AI systems intervene by modifying stimulation rather than stopping it abruptly. Tasks slow, sensory input softens, and demands recalibrate. These adjustments signal safety to the nervous system, allowing parasympathetic pathways to reengage. Over time, repeated exposure to these regulated transitions trains the brain to shift states more fluidly, reducing the duration and intensity of stress responses.

Recovery is not passive; it is an active neurological process. During periods of rest, the brain consolidates learning, clears metabolic waste, and stabilizes synaptic changes. AI systems optimize recovery by aligning cognitive demand with biological rhythms. Activity is scheduled when neural readiness is high, and restoration is encouraged when capacity wanes. This alignment prevents burnout while preserving momentum, allowing neuroplastic gains to compound rather than erode.

Sleep is central to nervous system reset, and AI-guided neuroplasticity increasingly incorporates sleep architecture into its models. By correlating cognitive performance with sleep quality, AI systems adjust learning intensity to avoid interfering with consolidation phases. This integration recognizes that adaptation does not occur solely during effort, but during recovery that follows.

Another critical function of AI-assisted stabilization is reducing allostatic load—the cumulative burden of stress on neural systems. By preventing prolonged activation, AI limits wear on emotional, cognitive, and physiological circuits. This protection preserves plasticity across the lifespan, supporting longevity rather than short-term optimization.

As stabilization improves, the brain regains flexibility. Transitions between focus and rest become smoother. Emotional responses resolve more quickly. Cognitive clarity persists longer. These outcomes are not isolated benefits; they reflect a nervous system that trusts its ability to recover. That trust is essential for exploration, learning, and adaptation.

The ultimate aim of AI-guided nervous system regulation is resilience rather than avoidance. A resilient brain can engage deeply, recover fully, and reengage without accumulating damage. Artificial intelligence supports this cycle by managing thresholds the brain cannot reliably track on its own. Over time, regulation becomes internalized, reducing dependence on external systems.

This chapter completes the foundational arc of Book 1. Neuroplasticity flourishes when attention is trained, memory reinforced, emotions regulated, habits repatterned, and the nervous system stabilized. AI's greatest contribution is not accelerating any single function, but orchestrating them into a coherent, sustainable system. With stabilization achieved, the brain is prepared for the deeper healing and recovery explored in the next book of this series.

"The Moment the Noise Settled"

For years, Caleb thought exhaustion was the price of ambition. His mind never stopped. Ideas collided, responsibilities overlapped, and rest felt like failure. Even when he slept, he woke tense, as if something unresolved followed him into the night. He assumed this was simply how modern life worked.

When Caleb began using an AI-guided nervous system program, he expected productivity tools. Instead, the system seemed uninterested in output. It tracked his patterns quietly—when his focus fractured, when his reactions sharpened, when fatigue lingered longer than effort justified.

The changes were subtle. Sessions ended sooner than expected. Notifications softened. Silence appeared where stimulation once lived. At first, Caleb resisted. Slowing down felt uncomfortable, almost threatening. But the system adjusted gradually, never forcing rest—only inviting it. One evening, after a demanding day, Caleb noticed something unfamiliar. His body relaxed without instruction. His thoughts slowed naturally. There was no crash, no collapse—just settling. The tension he carried daily loosened without effort.

Weeks passed, and the settling became familiar. Stress still arose, but it no longer lingered. Recovery felt accessible. Sleep deepened. Focus returned without strain. The AI system intervened less often now; Caleb's nervous system had learned the rhythm.

One afternoon, while sitting quietly between tasks, Caleb realized the noise that once filled every moment had receded. In its place was clarity—not forced, not fragile, but stable. His mind felt spacious, capable of effort without urgency.

Caleb understood then that rest was not the opposite of productivity. It was the condition that made productivity sustainable. The AI hadn't slowed him down. It had taught his nervous system how to come home.

Chapter 8

Creativity, Insight, and AI-Guided Expansion of Cognitive Flexibility

Creativity is not a rare talent reserved for a few, nor is it a spontaneous burst that arrives without cause. It is a neurological process that emerges when the brain can move fluidly between networks, allowing ideas to combine, dissolve, and recombine in novel ways. At its core, creativity depends on cognitive flexibility—the ability to shift perspective, explore uncertainty, and tolerate ambiguity without shutting down. Artificial intelligence enhances this capacity not by generating ideas for the brain, but by expanding the conditions under which insight becomes possible.

The creative brain relies on a delicate balance between structure and freedom. Too much control suppresses exploration, while too little coherence produces noise. AI systems excel at maintaining this balance by dynamically adjusting constraints. When the brain becomes rigid, AI introduces variation. When it becomes scattered, AI provides gentle structure. This oscillation strengthens neural pathways that support flexible thinking, allowing creativity to emerge reliably rather than sporadically. Insight often arises when the brain disengages from linear problem-solving and enters associative mode. In this state, disparate neural networks communicate more freely, enabling unexpected connections. AI-guided systems recognize when the brain is primed for this transition by monitoring cognitive markers such as response variability, pattern divergence, and attentional drift. Rather than forcing focus, AI allows controlled looseness, creating space for insight to surface.

Artificial intelligence also expands creativity by reducing fear-based inhibition. Many creative blocks originate not from lack of ideas, but from premature evaluation. The brain's threat networks suppress exploration when outcomes feel uncertain or risky. AI systems mitigate this by separating ideation from judgment. Early stages are structured to encourage quantity and variation without consequence, while refinement occurs later under different conditions. This sequencing retrains the brain to explore without self-censorship.

Cognitive flexibility strengthens when the brain practices switching between modes of thinking. AI systems facilitate this practice by alternating tasks that require divergent thinking with those that demand convergence. Over time, transitions between modes become smoother, reducing mental friction. The brain learns that flexibility is safe and productive, weakening rigid patterns that limit creative range. Another dimension of AI-enhanced creativity is exposure to controlled novelty. The brain requires new stimuli to form new associations, but excessive novelty overwhelms processing. AI curates novelty at an optimal rate, introducing unfamiliar elements gradually and contextually. This pacing allows the brain to integrate new information without destabilization, fostering innovation grounded in understanding rather than chaos.

AI also supports creativity by mapping individual cognitive styles. Some brains generate ideas rapidly but struggle with refinement. Others produce fewer ideas but excel at depth. By recognizing these tendencies, AI tailors creative environments that complement strengths while gently developing weaker capacities. This personalization prevents comparison-driven inhibition and encourages authentic creative expression.

As creative flexibility increases, broader cognitive benefits emerge. Problem-solving becomes more adaptive. Emotional resilience improves as the brain tolerates uncertainty more easily. Learning accelerates because new information finds multiple points of entry into existing networks. Creativity thus becomes a functional advantage rather than an abstract quality.

The long-term impact of AI-guided creativity is not dependence on external generation, but internal expansion. The brain becomes more willing to explore, less threatened by ambiguity, and more capable of synthesizing complex information. Artificial intelligence does not replace imagination; it strengthens the neural conditions that allow imagination to flourish.

This chapter reframes creativity as a trainable aspect of neuroplasticity. By guiding flexibility rather than dictating output, AI helps the brain rediscover its capacity for insight. With creative networks expanded, the mind becomes not only more inventive, but more adaptable—ready to navigate complexity with curiosity rather than resistance.

"When the Answer Didn't Arrive Whole"

Sofia had always waited for certainty. She believed good ideas arrived fully formed, clean and obvious. When they didn't, she assumed she lacked creativity. Problems lingered unresolved because she searched for the perfect solution before moving forward.

When Sofia began working with an AI-guided creative system, she expected suggestions, templates, maybe even answers. Instead, the system asked her to explore. Prompts arrived incomplete. Directions shifted unexpectedly. At first, this frustrated her. She wanted clarity, not ambiguity.

But the system adjusted its pace. When Sofia hesitated, it offered another angle. When she overanalyzed, it loosened constraints. There was no pressure to be right—only to continue. Gradually, she noticed something unfamiliar: curiosity without anxiety.

Ideas began arriving in fragments. Instead of dismissing them, Sofia allowed them to linger. The system encouraged variation, not evaluation. Over time, fragments connected. Patterns emerged where none had existed. The fear of being wrong softened.

One afternoon, while working on a long-standing problem, Sofia realized the solution wasn't arriving as a single insight. It was forming slowly, through accumulation. She didn't rush to name it. She let it develop.

Days later, the idea crystallized—not as a revelation, but as a recognition. It felt earned, integrated, real. Sofia understood then that creativity wasn't about brilliance. It was about allowing the mind to wander without getting lost.

The AI system faded into the background as her confidence grew. She no longer waited for certainty to begin. She trusted the process of exploration. Her brain had learned that answers could arrive incomplete—and that was enough.

Chapter 9

Brain Longevity, Cognitive Aging, and AI-Driven Neuroprotection

Cognitive aging is not a sudden event, nor is it an inevitable decline that begins at a fixed age. It is a gradual process shaped by cumulative stress, inflammation, metabolic health, neural efficiency, and the ongoing use—or disuse—of cognitive networks. The brain does not fail all at once; it narrows. Pathways that are repeatedly engaged remain robust, while those neglected weaken over time. Artificial intelligence offers a powerful intervention at this stage of life by shifting brain aging from passive deterioration to active neuroprotection.

One of the most significant contributors to cognitive decline is reduced neural diversity. As routines solidify and novelty decreases, the brain relies on fewer pathways to accomplish daily tasks. This efficiency conserves energy in the short term but limits adaptability over time. AI systems counteract this narrowing by introducing structured novelty that encourages continued network engagement without overwhelming the brain. By varying cognitive challenges, contexts, and modalities, AI keeps neural systems flexible, preserving plasticity well into later life. Inflammation and metabolic stress also play critical roles in brain aging. Chronic stress, poor sleep, and cognitive overload disrupt the brain's maintenance processes, accelerating wear on neural circuits. AI-guided systems detect early signs of strain through performance variability, reaction slowing, and attentional instability. By adjusting cognitive demand and recovery cycles, AI reduces cumulative stress on the brain, preserving functional capacity over time.

Another key factor in longevity is error correction. Aging brains often struggle not because they cannot learn, but because they are less efficient at identifying and correcting subtle mistakes. AI systems provide immediate, low-friction feedback that strengthens error-detection networks. This ongoing calibration maintains accuracy and confidence, preventing the compounding effects of small cognitive slips that often erode performance with age.

Memory preservation is central to neuroprotection. Rather than focusing solely on recall, AI systems reinforce memory networks by encouraging integration. Information is connected across domains, contexts, and emotional states, strengthening retrieval pathways. This distributed encoding protects memories from decay by embedding them within broader neural frameworks rather than isolating them as fragile units.

AI also supports longevity by maintaining executive function. Decision-making, planning, and self-monitoring decline when cognitive load exceeds capacity. AI reduces this burden by managing complexity externally, allowing the brain to focus on higher-order reasoning. Over time, this preservation of executive resources supports independence, adaptability, and confidence.

Importantly, AI-driven neuroprotection is proactive rather than reactive. Instead of waiting for decline to become apparent, AI monitors baseline performance and intervenes early. Small adjustments made consistently prevent larger disruptions later. This preventative approach reframes aging not as loss, but as maintenance—a process of sustaining what already exists through intelligent stewardship.

Emotional health is another pillar of cognitive longevity. Depression, isolation, and chronic anxiety accelerate neural decline by reducing engagement and motivation. AI systems promote emotional resilience by encouraging meaningful interaction, curiosity, and purposeful activity. These experiences stimulate dopamine and serotonin pathways that support both mood and plasticity.

The cumulative effect of these interventions is a brain that remains engaged with life. Curiosity persists. Learning continues. Adaptation feels possible. Artificial intelligence does not halt aging, but it reshapes how aging unfolds—slowing decline by preserving the conditions that allow the brain to remain plastic.

This chapter reframes longevity as an active process rather than a defensive one. AI-guided neuroprotection empowers individuals to participate in their cognitive future, reinforcing the idea that mental vitality is not defined by age, but by engagement. With neuroprotective foundations established, the brain remains capable of growth, meaning, and connection across the lifespan.

"What Still Grew"

Margaret noticed the changes quietly. Names took longer to surface. Directions required more concentration. She adapted without complaint, telling herself it was normal, that nothing was truly wrong. But beneath acceptance was a subtle grief—the sense that her mind was slowly closing doors.

When her daughter introduced her to an AI-guided cognitive program, Margaret was skeptical. She didn't want to "train" her brain. She wanted to live. The system surprised her by focusing not on improvement, but on engagement. It offered puzzles that felt like invitations, not tests. Conversations unfolded at her pace. Nothing rushed her. At first, Margaret worried she was failing. Tasks shifted when she hesitated, but without judgment. Over time, she realized the system wasn't measuring what she couldn't do—it was reinforcing what she still could. Each interaction felt respectful, almost companionable.

Weeks passed, and Margaret noticed subtle changes. She felt more alert during conversations. Reading became enjoyable again. Curiosity returned—not forced, but genuine. She found herself wondering about things she hadn't considered in years.

One afternoon, while teaching her grandson a card game, Margaret realized she was fully present. There was no effort, no self-monitoring. Just participation. The moment felt ordinary—and precious.

The AI system faded gradually into the background. Margaret didn't rely on it daily anymore. Its influence lingered in the way she approached life—with openness rather than caution. Her mind felt spacious again, not because it was younger, but because it was engaged.

Margaret understood then that longevity wasn't about holding on to the past. It was about continuing to grow, even slowly. Her brain hadn't been preserved like a museum piece. It had been invited to remain alive.

Chapter 10

The Integrated AI-Powered Brain: From Adaptation to Human Evolution

Neuroplasticity is not a single process but a coordinated system of change that unfolds across attention, memory, emotion, behavior, creativity, recovery, and longevity. Throughout this book, each of these elements has been explored individually, yet the true transformation occurs when they operate together as an integrated whole. The AI-powered brain is not defined by any one capability, but by the harmony between systems that once functioned in isolation. Artificial intelligence accelerates this integration by synchronizing neural change across domains, allowing the brain to adapt not in fragments, but as a living, coherent system.

The human brain evolved to survive in environments far less complex than those it now inhabits. Modern cognitive strain is not the result of weakness, but of mismatch. The brain is asked to process volumes of information, emotional input, and decision-making demands that exceed its evolutionary design. AI does not alter the brain's biology, but it compensates for this mismatch by acting as an external regulator—filtering noise, pacing demand, and guiding recovery so the brain can function optimally within modern conditions.

When AI systems coordinate attention training with memory reinforcement, emotional regulation with habit repatterning, and creativity with nervous system recovery, the brain experiences change as continuity rather than disruption. This coordination prevents the common failure mode of self-improvement efforts, where gains in one area are undermined by neglect in another. AI ensures that progress compounds rather than conflicts, stabilizing growth across time.

The integrated brain becomes more predictive than reactive. Instead of responding to overload after it occurs, the system anticipates strain and adjusts conditions preemptively. This predictive regulation represents a fundamental shift in human cognition. The brain is no longer forced to operate at the edge of breakdown to grow. Growth becomes sustainable, measured, and aligned with long-term health.

Importantly, AI does not replace self-awareness—it cultivates it. By reflecting cognitive and emotional patterns back to the individual consistently, AI trains the brain to recognize itself. Over time, this reflection internalizes. The brain learns its rhythms, limits, and strengths. What begins as external guidance becomes embodied intelligence.

The result is not dependence on technology, but liberation from unconscious patterns. The AI-powered brain is more autonomous, not less. It wastes less energy on correction, conflict, and recovery because it has learned to self-regulate efficiently. This efficiency creates space for meaning, creativity, and connection—capacities often diminished by chronic cognitive overload.

As this integration stabilizes, a subtle shift occurs in identity. Individuals no longer experience themselves as fighting their own minds. Thought, emotion, and behavior align more naturally. Effort is still required, but it is purposeful rather than draining. The brain becomes a collaborator rather than an obstacle.

This is the threshold between adaptation and evolution. Adaptation restores function. Evolution expands possibility. AI-guided neuroplasticity does not merely repair what is broken—it establishes conditions under which the brain can continue to evolve throughout life. Learning does not end. Healing does not plateau. Growth does not expire.

The future of the human brain is not artificial. It is augmented—supported by systems that respect biology rather than override it. Artificial intelligence becomes most powerful when it disappears into the background, leaving behind a brain that is more resilient, flexible, and self-aware than before. This final chapter completes Book 1 by closing the loop. Neuroplasticity is no longer an abstract concept. It is a lived process, guided intelligently, sustained ethically, and integrated holistically. With this foundation established, the next stage becomes possible: not just adaptation, but repair. The brain that has learned how to change is now ready to heal.

"The Mind That Stopped Resisting Itself"

Julian spent most of his life believing discipline meant force. He pushed through fatigue, ignored emotional signals, and optimized productivity wherever possible. His mind functioned—but always at a cost. Focus required tension. Rest felt undeserved. Growth came in bursts, followed by collapse.

When Julian began interacting with an AI-guided cognitive system, he expected efficiency. What he encountered instead was alignment. The system did not reward pushing harder. It rewarded balance. When he tried to override exhaustion, the system slowed. When he disengaged too early, it gently challenged him. There was no judgment—only response.

At first, Julian felt exposed. The system noticed things he had ignored for years: when his attention fractured, when stress lingered, when habits activated automatically. He couldn't argue with the data. But instead of feeling controlled, he felt seen. Weeks passed, and resistance softened. Julian stopped fighting the adjustments. He allowed the system to guide pacing, recovery, and challenge. Something unexpected happened. His mind began cooperating. Focus arrived without tension. Ideas formed without pressure. Rest restored rather than interrupted.

The changes extended beyond cognition. His conversations slowed. His reactions softened. Decisions became clearer. The internal conflict that once defined his effort faded. His brain no longer felt like a machine to be managed, but a system to be understood.

One afternoon, while reflecting quietly, Julian realized he wasn't thinking about optimization at all. He was present. The constant negotiation with his own limits had ended. There was effort—but no resistance.

Over time, the AI system intervened less frequently. Its role diminished as Julian's brain internalized the patterns. He no longer needed reminders to pause or refocus. His nervous system knew when to recover. His habits aligned naturally with his goals.

Julian understood then that intelligence wasn't about control. It was about coherence. His mind hadn't become stronger by force—it had become integrated through understanding. The technology hadn't changed who he was. It had removed the friction that prevented him from becoming himself

Epilogue

The Brain That Knows It Can Change

This book began with a simple but transformative truth: the brain is not fixed. It never was. What artificial intelligence has revealed is not a new capacity, but a forgotten one—the brain's lifelong ability to adapt, rewire, and heal when given the right conditions. Neuroplasticity is not a miracle reserved for rare cases or extraordinary effort. It is the brain's default mode when it feels safe, supported, and engaged. AI's role is not to replace human intelligence, but to restore the environments that allow it to flourish.

Across these chapters, the brain has been explored not as a machine to be optimized, but as a living system that responds to rhythm, feedback, and care. Attention sharpened when demand aligned with capacity. Memory strengthened when reinforcement respected timing. Emotion stabilized when the nervous system learned it could recover. Habits shifted when new pathways became easier than old ones. Creativity expanded when fear loosened its grip. Longevity emerged not from resisting aging, but from remaining engaged with life. None of these changes occurred through force. They occurred through alignment. Artificial intelligence succeeds where so many self-improvement efforts fail because it does not ask the brain to override itself. It listens. It responds. It adjusts. In doing so, it teaches the brain how to do the same. What begins as external guidance becomes internal wisdom. The brain learns its own signals, thresholds, and recovery cycles. Eventually, the system steps back, leaving behind a mind that understands itself more clearly than before.

The most important shift introduced in this book is not technological—it is relational. The relationship between a person and their own mind changes. The brain is no longer something to battle, discipline, or mistrust. It becomes something to collaborate with. This shift alone reduces enormous cognitive and emotional strain. Energy once spent on internal conflict becomes available for growth, meaning, and connection.

Neuroplasticity guided by AI is not about constant improvement. It is about sustainability. A brain that can change without breaking is a brain that can heal. The practices described throughout this book lay the groundwork for recovery from injury, trauma, and disease—not by promising instant repair, but by restoring the conditions under which repair becomes possible. Healing is not a separate process from learning; it is learning applied to recovery. As this book closes, it is important to recognize that awareness itself is a form of plasticity. Simply knowing that the brain can change alters how it responds to challenge. Hope is not abstract—it is neurological. When the brain expects adaptability, it engages differently. AI reinforces this expectation by providing evidence, feedback, and continuity. Over time, belief becomes embodied experience.

The future described here is not distant. It is already unfolding quietly in therapeutic settings, learning environments, and daily life. The greatest impact of AI on the human brain will not be dramatic interfaces or digital minds. It will be the quiet normalization of growth at every stage of life. Change will no longer feel exceptional. It will feel natural.

This epilogue does not mark an ending, but a threshold. The brain that understands it can change is no longer limited by fear of stagnation. It is ready to repair what has been damaged, restore what has been lost, and reimagine what is possible. The next book begins where this one leaves off—not with potential, but with healing.

"After the Struggle Ended"

For most of his life, Thomas believed his mind was something to endure. He worked around it, compensated for it, pushed through its limits. When things went wrong—burnout, anxiety, lapses in memory—he blamed himself. He assumed decline was personal failure.

Thomas encountered AI-guided neuroplastic training at a point when effort no longer worked. He didn't seek transformation. He sought relief. The system didn't offer promises. It offered presence. It responded when he slowed. It eased when he strained. It waited when he resisted.

At first, Thomas felt disoriented. Without struggle, he didn't know how to measure progress. There was no heroic effort, no dramatic breakthrough. Change arrived quietly. His mind felt less crowded. His reactions softened. Sleep deepened. He stopped bracing himself for the day.

Weeks passed, and Thomas noticed something subtle but profound. He trusted his mind again. When fatigue appeared, he responded rather than pushed. When emotions rose, they passed without leaving damage. When learning challenged him, he stayed with it instead of withdrawing.

The system intervened less often now. Thomas didn't notice when it stopped adjusting things in the background. He had internalized the rhythm. His brain recognized its own needs. The struggle that once defined his effort dissolved—not because life became easier, but because resistance ended.

One morning, while sitting quietly with a cup of coffee, Thomas realized he felt whole. Not optimized. Not perfected. Just whole. His mind wasn't something he managed anymore.

It was something he lived in.

He understood then that healing hadn't come from fixing himself. It had come from stopping the fight. The AI hadn't changed his brain. It had shown his brain how to stop being at war with itself.

And in that peace, change finally stayed.

www.ingramcontent.com/pod-product-compliance
Ingram Content Group UK Ltd.
Pitfield, Milton Keynes, MK11 3LW, UK
UKHW020155290926
15471UKWH00005B/893

9 798295 622496